This Book Belongs To

Includes 100 adorable fairy and fantasy coloring images from these four signature titles by Selina Fenech.

As an artist, color is a thing of magic in my life. Color creates shapes, forms, and feelings in the artworks I paint. Laying color onto a blank page is when I feel closest to true magic, when I feel happiest and most relaxed, and it's through what I create that I share my love of magic with the world. Through my coloring books I want to share that same magic with you.

Happy coloring! ~ Selina XOX

See more art and coloring fun at
www.selinafenech.com

Faedorables - Coloring Collection
by Selina Fenech
First Published November 2019
Published by Fairies and Fantasy PTY LTD
ISBN: 978-0-6487080-1-8

Getting the Most from this Book

Turn off and move away from distractions. Relax into the peaceful process of coloring and enjoy the magic of these fantasy images.

Experiment! There is no right or wrong way to color, just have fun.

This book works best with color pencils or markers. Wet mediums should be used sparingly. Slip a piece of card behind the image you're working on in case the markers bleed through.

Don't be scared to dismantle this book. Cut finished pages out to frame, or split the book so you and a loved one can color together.

Never run out of fantasy coloring pages by signing up to Selina's newsletter. Get free downloadable pages and updates on new books at - selinafenech.com/free-coloring-sampler/

Share Your Work

Share on Instagram with #colorselina to be included in Selina's coloring gallery, and visit the gallery for inspiration.

selinafenech.com/coloringgallery

"Flower Fairy"

"Summer Friends"

"Buzzy Buddies"

"Enchanted BFFs"

"Witchy Friends"

"Littlest Friends"

"Smokey Kisses"

"Book of Magic"

"Spring Playtime"

"Day Dreaming Aloft"

"First Kiss"

"Sweetest Dreams"

"A Perfect Day"

"Clamshell Clan"

"Cupcake Fairy"

"Baby Dragon Cuddles"

"Winter Friends"

"Autumn Wonder"

"The Newest Fairy"

"Unicorn and Maiden"

"Sleepy Star Fairy"

"Off to Make Magic"

"Little Princess"

"Cuppa Mermaid"

"Basket of Joy"

"Cait Sidhe"

"Hippocampus"

"Alicorn"

"Selkie"

"Wolpertinger"

"Cockatrice"

"Dryad and Tree-man"

"Satyr"

"Chimera"

"Naiad and Kelpie"

"Pegasus and Centaur"

"Kitsune"

"Griffin"

"Sphinx"

"Dragon"

"Drop Bear and Bunyip"

"Unicorn"

"Gargoyle and Demon"

"Kludde and Vampire"

"Kraken"

"Yeti"

"Nessy"

"Hydra"

"*Phoenix*"

"Quetzalcoatl"

"Thinking of Tea"

"Just Me and My Tea"

"Decorating"

"Nice Hot Bath"

"Tea and Roses"

"Love a Hot Tea"

"High Tea Uni"

"Mine!"

"Tea Delivery"

"Dragon Tea"

"Tea with Friends"

"Underwater Tea Party"

"Two Cups, Please."

"Perfect Night In"

"Just One More Cup."

"But We'll Be Late!"

"Magical Cuppa"

"Cupcake Dreams"

"Splashing in the Bath"

"Hop Out of My Tea This Instant"

"Icing on the Cake"

"Witchy Tea Friends"

"Tea on a Toadstool"

"Cupcake Hair, Don't Care"

"Marie AnTEAoinette"

"Morning Magic"

"Voodoo"

"A Spell of Threes"

"Brains"

"Dragon Queen"

"Chain of Skulls"

"Darkling"

"Electricity"

"Headless Horsewoman"

"Vampy Friends"

"Fading Away"

"Little Devil"

"Medusa"

"*Melody Dark*"

"Miss Muffet"

"Mummy's Curse"

"Nice Night for Flying"

"Night's Companions"

"Wolf Pack"

"Persephone and Cerberus"

"Pretty Dolly"

"Pumpkin Patch Cats"

"Putting You Back Together"

"Reaper"

"Siren Song"

"Witching Hour"

COLORING BOOKS

BY SELINA FENECH

So much more magic to color!

With over 100,000 copies sold, there are more than 25 coloring titles o explore your creativity through in Selina fenech's bestselling coloring range.

Themed signature range, Faedorables range, pocket sized editions, grayscale editions, coloring journals, and bundle collections.

Try out some mini samples on the following pages.

Discover more at www.selinafenech.com

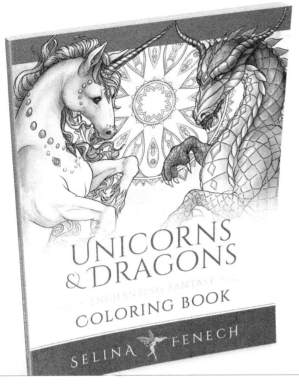

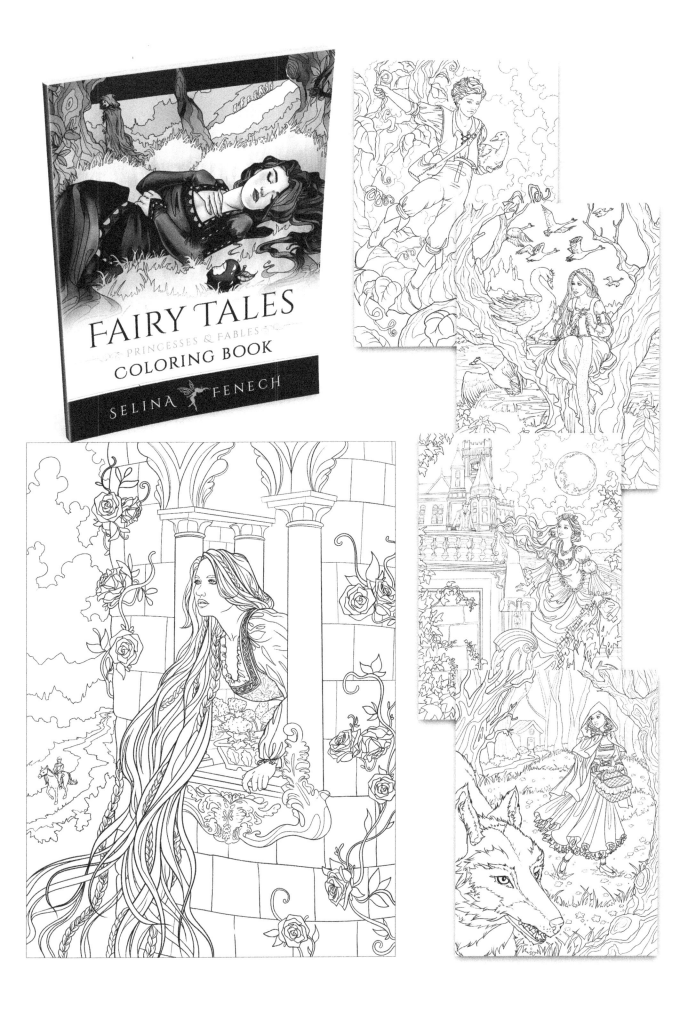

About the Artist

As a lover of all things fantasy, Selina has made a living as an artist since she was 23 years old selling her magical creations. Her works range from oil paintings to oracle decks, dolls to digital scrapbooking, plus Young Adult novels, jewelry, and coloring books.

Born in 1981 to Australian and Maltese parents, Selina lives in Australia with her husband, daughter, and growing urban farm menagerie.

Download printable coloring pages from all of Selina's coloring books at www.etsy.com/shop/printablefantasy

See all of Selina's bestselling coloring books, journals, art books and more at amazon.com/author/selina

Sneak a peek into Selina's studio and see what she's working on now at instagram.com/selinafenech/

Get social with Selina and see how others are coloring her work in her coloring group at bit.ly/colorselina

Made in the USA
Las Vegas, NV
10 May 2024